Being 'Good':
An Ontological View of Ethics

Being 'Good':
An Ontological View of Ethics

Karim Lahham

TABAH RESEARCH

KALAM RESEARCH & MEDIA

TABAH ESSAYS SERIES | NUMBER 6 | 2017
ISSN: 3399-2017

Being 'Good': An Ontological View of Ethics
ISBN: 978-9948-00-093-8

Tabah Essays consist of shorter, more informal conceptual presentations that focus on the elucidation of ideas to inform and stimulate new Islamic perspectives on the world.

Cover Image © by Pedro Rufo / Shutterstock.com
This work was originally presented as a paper at the Kalam Research and Media Ethics Working Group Workshop, the Alliance of Civilizations Institute at the Fatih Sultan Mehmet University, Istanbul, 10-11 May 2014. The workshop was funded, in part, by the Templeton Foundation.

Summary

This paper sets out to explore several dimensions of the science of 'ethics', but above all to frame it as a science of the soul, within the context of a 'meta-ethical' discourse. By paying particular attention to the role of an integral metaphysics within the ambit of the classification of the sciences, it seeks to both determine the parameters of ethics and also underline the relationship between modes of being and modes of action. This relationship is further explored within the context of passages from Muhyī al-Dīn Ibn 'Arabī's *Futūhāt*. An approach to ethics from a metaphysical point of view, in the Akbarian sense, serves to establish that the ontological approach to ethics is firmly rooted in our tradition, one that is premised on a transcendental definition of the human being. Modern ethics, in contrast, is characterized by an inability to transcend the imposture of a pragmatic psychologism. Right ethics in this scheme, therefore, stems from right theology, in turn providing a right economics and thus ensuring a right politics, when premises are declared, certain, and founded on an ontological order of reality.

About the Author

KARIM LAHHAM, MA (RCA), MA (OXON.), PHD (CANTAB.), Barrister-at-Law of the Inner Temple. He is the author of, inter alia, *The Roman Catholic Church's Position on Islam After Vatican II; Muhammad Shahrur's 'Cargo Cult'; Metaphysics and Sociology; and Gandhi, Islam, and the Principles of Non-violence and Attachment to Truth.*

'The more real
          one is
the less evil
          one becomes.'
—page 15

INTRODUCTION

The science of ethics, in accordance with such diverse thinkers from different ends of the philosophical spectrum, such as Naṣīr al-Dīn Ṭūsī or Ibn ʿArabī, is above all a science of the soul. It is precisely that science that investigates how one can attain a disposition of the soul to secure right action and discern the wrongful act. This paper will attempt to explore several dimensions of this within the context of the 'meta-ethical' discussion, itself a neo-analytical term of art with its own conceptual history and implications. This paper will focus particularly on the rightful role of metaphysics within the ambit of the classification of the sciences to determine the parameters of ethics but more importantly to understand the relationship between modes of being and modes of action. This will be clarified in the context of some passages from Muḥyī al-Dīn Ibn ʿArabī's *Futūḥāt* in the latter half of the paper.

It might be useful to start by examining some pertinent aspects of the nature of meta-ethical discourse, and by outlining in general terms the relationship between meta-ethics and normative ethics in analytic systems. It can be stated that meta-ethics is concerned with the analysis of ethical expressions, their meanings, and logical functions. As the theories of logical positivism have now been safely discarded (and there is nothing more old-fashioned than the former avant-garde) it can also now be safely denied that sentences and propositions can be reduced to basic facts in the real order. The clarification of language, though, has itself become the end rather than the means to an end, and thus meaning is held to be dependent on the way language is used (the late Wittgenstein). Words no longer point beyond themselves but are merely referents to the function that terms have in a proposition. Metaphysics as an explanation of the real, even if the latter is experienced, has become impossible. Language and thought are synonymous, and philosophy clarifies thought by clarifying the terms used. On this reading, a proposition can say nothing about reality, as its meaningfulness is derived from the intrinsic relationship of its terms[1].

It is in this somewhat reductionist ambience that meta-ethics is posited. The term was first coined in 1949 by A. J. Ayer to name his new approach to moral philosophy, building on what was largely imported from the Vienna Circle upon his return to England in the early 1930s.[2] If normative ethics was the consideration of whether particular acts are morally wrong or right, meta-ethics is the consideration of the meaning, nature, and justification of normative judgments. Thus McCloskey characteristically states that there is an apparent uncertainty among

---

1. See J. O. Urmson, *Philosophical Analysis* (Oxford: Clarendon Press, 1958).
2. See A. J. Ayer, 'On Analysis of Moral Judgments', *Horizon* 20, no. 117 (Septem-ber 1949), 182.

meta-ethicists concerning the nature of meta-ethics itself, as it tends to conform to the meta-ethical theory held by a particular proponent. We can see dimly the return of culture-relative categorizations here, in that ethical codes are perceived largely as culture-relative and are often the underlying reason why the notion of absolute understandings for good and bad is rejected by modern societies.

McCloskey further states that the function of meta-ethics, following what was outlined earlier, could be said to be the discovery of the meanings of ethical terms, adding rather less lucidly: 'Thus the meta-ethical theory that is arrived at tends to colour the account given of the nature of meta-ethics.'[3] So utilitarianism may be viewed as a normative ethic if viewed as a series of moral judgments that express moral points of view through philosophical activity. Utilitarianism, however, on the above reading, can also be viewed as a meta-ethic if the activity is based on the definitions of the good and the bad. In other words, meta-ethics is not always normatively neutral and can, as in this case, entail normative conclusions. The line of separation is rather blurred as admitted by von Wright[4] and, I contend, thus affects the regulative authority required of a meta-ethic. This is because the implication is that meta-ethicists will make normative judgments in selecting which facts to explain, in the sense that they determine what a moral discourse needs to possess as essential features.

---

3. H. J. McCloskey, *Meta-Ethics and Normative Ethics* (The Hague: Martinus Nijhoff, 1969), 3.
4. G. H. von Wright, *The Varieties of Goodness* (London: Routledge & Kegan Paul, 1963), 2–3.

Does this not beg the question, though, of how one is supposed to arrive at a regulative and authoritative meta-ethic in the first place, and on what basis it can be grounded? Should one be speaking of a meta-meta-ethic in that case, and if so in infinite regress? This is in line with the lack of clarity one also finds in the ethical discourses of analytic philosophers such as Charles Stevenson, Stephen Toulmin, and Stuart Hampshire, a lack of clarity engendered largely by the absence of an integral metaphysics.

The naturalistic fallacy set out in the first chapter of G. E. Moore's *Principia Ethica* (1903)[5] consisted in stating that the notion of goodness or moral value per se could not correspond with anything ordinary (or properties) found in nature.[6] The fallacy is in attempting to pass from the fact that something is natural to the fact that it is good, from the 'is' to the 'ought'. Thus Moore contended that conventional ethics confused ethical facts with natural facts. The early Wittgenstein together with the logical positivists believed that ethical statements could not be verified, since to do so, the statement would have to be reduced to something else first. The latter concluded that there was no way, therefore, of verifying ethical facts. Moore, on the other hand, differed by claiming that goodness was a fact, an indefinable fact such as yellow, but was nevertheless recognizable when seen. As the colour yellow could be correlated with certain

<hr>

5. G. E. Moore, Principia Ethica (Cambridge: Cambridge University Press, 1903), 10 et seq

6. The idea here being that moral distinctions have no ontological status, one that goes back to David Hume, *A Treatise of Human Nature*, ed. L. A. Selby-Bigge (Oxford: Clarendon Press, 1888), 469.

light vibrations, which do not define it nor could be considered as the colour itself, so too one may correlate the good with pleasure or utility, without the latter defining the good or being identical with it.[7] One may say 'pleasure is good' but one does not mean pleasure *means* good.

Although Moore as an intuitionist considers the good indefinable as a quality, he sets out in the first two chapters of his *Ethics* a utilitarian and consequentialist formula. He states there that our duty is to perform an act that is the most conducive to the production of the good. The only valid criterion ultimately here for Moore is an investigation of the consequences that such an act will produce. The impasse of a consequentialist position, however, is precisely that an immediate effect of an act may be wrong but its future effect may be right and vice versa. How then can one judge the goodness of the act? In answer, Moore posits here an objective right and a subjective right. When the total effects of an act are not better than the total effects of an alternative act which could have been per-formed, then that act is objectively wrong. Subjective wrong, on the other hand, is when the blameworthiness of an act can be determined on the basis of foreseeable consequences. The former objectivity criteria are impossible to calculate, as is the subjective and arbitrary notion of the 'foreseeable' as a basis for setting out any rule of morality.

For Stevenson, who followed Moore's path while moving away from Ayer's intolerant positivism, ethical statements do have meaning but a combined

---

7. Moore, *Principia Ethica*, 6–17.

factual and emotive meaning.[8] An ethical statement for Stevenson, being a quasi-imperative command, elicits not only the statement x is good, but also that I approve of x and you should approve of x too. This demand for approval is what he means by the emotive meaning. Stevenson defends his scheme from a charge of irrationality by stating clearly that reasons may be given for approval or dis-approval and that such reasons must have logical consistency and thus rationality. The fact, however, that reasons may be given for ethical judgments surely cannot absolve Stevenson from irrationality, since logical consistency of reasoning cannot furnish a criterion of value. Logical consistency can tell me my proposition is correct, it cannot tell me whether my proposition is true. There is no recourse to first principles for Stevenson, and one is left with the irrationality of an ethical statement that is approved merely on the basis that one can furnish logically consistent reasons for approving it. It is irrational precisely because it obviates any moral system, since there can be no binding obligation when such obligation is based on personal choice.

Hampshire[9] and Toulmin[10] continue the line of Stevenson but with an added phenomenological bent, by examining ethical reasoning in an even more descriptive manner. Although both thinkers set out an examination of reasons for ethical judgments,

---

8. Charles Stevenson, *Ethics and Language* (New Haven: Yale University Press, 1944), 36.

9. Stuart Hampshire, *Thought and Action*, 2nd ed. (London: Chatto & Windus, 1982; 1959).

10. Stephen Toulmin, *An Examination of the Place of Reason in Ethics* (Cambridge: Cambridge University Press, 1950).

they nowhere provide any basis for justifying them nor whether one moral standard should be given pre-eminence over another. Although it could be said that in recent years the Analytic school has been moving steadily away from Ayer's positivism, a discernible residue nevertheless remains in its continued attachment to a latitudinarian descriptive approach to ethics. This is the key problem that brings us back to a type of moral relativism that cannot be mitigated seemingly by any application of an effective meta-ethic.

Ethics and Metaphysics

In a scheme of the classification of the sciences, whether that of Ibn Sīnā, Ghazālī,[11] or Tahānawī et al., the sciences are distinguished as either speculative (*nazarī*) or practical (*ʿamalī*). The speculative science is one whose fundamental purpose is the acquisition of knowledge as such, seeking the truth about its objects for the sake of truth alone. It is above all concerned with what those objects are and, therefore, concerned with their being. The practical science is also concerned with the truth of things but seeks to discover the rules and norms, which determine how an object ought to be. It is concerned fundamentally with the principles of regulation, which govern the correctness of acts in accordance with established norms.

The science of ethics (*akhlāq* or *ʿilm tahdhīb al-nafs* for Ghazālī) is deemed a practical science, and as with any science, is endowed with a particular

---

11. See his *Mizān al-ʿamal* (Cairo: Dār al-Maʿārif, 1380/1961), 230–2.

mawḍū, particular *masāʾil*, and *mabādī*.[12] According to Ibn Sīnā,[13] and his commentator Fakhr al-Dīn al-Rāzī, the *mabādī* (principles) of ethics as well as their teleology are revealed to the prophets. The prophets instruct those they have been sent to, of the perfection or completeness of actions. Rāzī further states that they do this in a universal way, as one who might seek a benefit may be guided to a particular course of action. This is in contradistinction to specifically guiding an individual such as Zayd in a particular and specific course of action.[14] The specificity of application of principle here is left largely to the determination of the *fuqahāʾ*, that is to say in accordance with practical reason. Rāzī makes an important point here, which Kant seemed unable to put into effect since the authority of morality, for him, resided in the autonomous will. The juxtaposition of a universal rule and a changing field of application could not be resolved by Kant on account of his positing the rightness of an action on the basis of whether it could be universalized or not.

In his *Critique of Practical Reason* (1788), Kant renders the universality and the necessity of the moral law dependent on a categorical imperative in our wills, and not on the empirical act and the end envisaged for the act.[15] These categorical imperatives impose themselves automatically as a priori forms of

---

12. Fārābī naturally includes ethics in his *Iḥṣāʾ al-ʿulūm* under *ʿilm al-siyāsāt*, but does not distinguish it by name as an independent science.

13. See Fakhr al-Dīn al-Rāzī, *Sharḥ ʿUyūn al-ḥikma*, ed. Aḥmad al-Saqqā (Tehran: Muʾassasat al-Ṣādiq, 1414/1994), 1:13–14.

14. Ibid., 14.

15. See Kant's *Critique of Practical Reason*, trans. Thomas Kingsmill Abbott, 3rd ed.(London: Longmans, Green & Co., 1883), 49–60.

the will and it is the imperatives that determine the empirical act and make it moral. It is the form of the will (the imperative), therefore, that makes the human act morally good. This imperative, which determines the good, is necessary and capable of universal application, so that all good actions can be universalized.

In accordance with this, one can continue to say that all that can be universalized must be right and good.[16] If the rightness of an action is its universality, following Kant, then the main problem we face is that all rules regarding right conduct have exceptions. For a universal rule to apply to more than one action these actions must be of the same kind without any extenuating circumstances to distinguish the application, or else a universal rule will be created for every type of such action. What we choose to will as a universal for Kant is dictated by our rational nature, that is to say, so long as what we wish to will as a universal is not inconsistent with itself.[17] Kant unsurprisingly conflates the objective basis of moral obligation with the subjective issue of explaining how what is obligatory can make a claim on us. Universality on its own, needless to say, cannot provide an adequate basis for understanding the rightness of a course of action and naturally so.

The traditional view of ethics, as a science, investigates human conduct from a perspective of right and wrong and not simply to provide a history of moral judgments or adumbrated customs. That is

---

16. The question surely should not be: can it be universalized? But rather, should it be universalized?

17. See Kant's *Critique*, 55.

to say that it directs and not merely describes human acts. The practical value being that it seeks to provide solutions and as such is, in effect, moral philosophy, as its goal is for the soul to reach *sa'āda*, the state of felicity, and thus an ontological state. The *minhāj* (method) of *akhlāq* can be stated as being threefold: the rational or speculative for arriving at right conduct; the casuistic method in passing judgment on individual moral cases; and the *iḥsānī* method, which has to do with the cultivation of virtues and *tahdhīb al-nafs*.[18]

All sciences, however, rest on certain postulates (*awḍā'*), which must be distinguished from hypotheses (*muṣādarāt*). Postulates are premises that are not self-evident necessarily, but are usually taken from other higher sciences wherein they have been proved. A hypothesis is that which is conceded without having been proved in another science, and indeed may not be capable of proof in the science in which it is being used. In one sense it is a presumption. The *awḍā'* of *'ilm al-akhlāq* can be said to be man's ability to reason (epistemological postulate), the existence of *al-Khāliq al-Bāri'* (theodicean postulate), and the existence of the soul (psychological postulate). Without these postulates no science of ethics is possible. The notion of *taklīf*, which incorporates the modern understanding of responsibility, incumbent on the Muslim, implies a *Mukallif*, the capacity to understand what is demanded of one, and finally the understanding that there is a soul subject to a final judgment.

---

18. For Ghazālī, ethics is essentially *'ilm aḥwāl al-qalb*.

A distinction at this juncture should be made between ethics and moral theology. In the Western tradition, ethics relies only on experience and the principles of reason and is thus a natural science, whereas moral theology derives its conclusions from principles of revelation and reason. On that basis the application of the name of ethics to *akhlāq* may potentially pose a problem. It may also be critical in ascertaining whether the use of terminology such as meta-ethic when discoursing on *akhlāq* is intellectually coherent.

The postulates referred to above are premises that are proven in the science of metaphysics *(al-ʿilm al-ilāhī)*, which has no postulates, as it is the science of first principles. Although the notion of first principles remains abhorred by the modern intellectual, following upon Kant and Hegel's reduction of metaphysics, the traditional view expressed here still pertains to the ahistoricity of metaphysics. The Nietzschian view that the truths of metaphysics are tied to history and thus are liable to change from one epoch to another, is one that rejects a permanent nature underlying the changing epochs.[19] The mutability of metaphysics, however, is a philosophical contention that seemingly must escape the historicist framework set out by Nietzsche and his successors in order for it to be a valid contention. If this is the case then the historicist view of metaphysics is not a necessary nor rational contention but one that is predicated on a pure voluntarism.

---

19. See Emil Fackenheim, *Metaphysics and Historicity* (Milwaukee: Marquette University Press, 1961); also F. Nietzsche, *The Will to Power*, trans. W. Kaufmann (New York: Random House, 1968).

In the tradition of Muḥyī al-Dīn Ibn ʿArabī, metaphysics is experiential, but not experimental, so that one can say that no other science or kind of knowledge is constitutive of metaphysics. It is as if Ibn ʿArabī holds to the view that it is not sufficient for one to conceptualize truth but rather one is called to become it. The present inversion of metaphysics, which is an inheritance of Kantian and Hegelian philosophies where the formal object of metaphysics is redacted, has led metaphysics to lose its autonomy as a theoretical science and furthermore to be used as a formal system reduced to an ideology. This also led in the nineteenth century to first principles becoming hypotheses, as the order of being gradually was reduced to the order of knowing and knowing reduced to making or doing. It is important to take note of this when engaging in contemporary discourse, should any successful comprehension of the traditional Islamic positions on ethics be ascertainable. The success or failure of the latter will depend on two major factors. The first is the extent to which the limitations of the contemporary mind regarding metaphysical thought can be mitigated. The second is the necessary curtailment of the use of Western correlative terms of art in Islamic discourse, as equivalent to the latter's terms on a basis of description alone.

THEOPHANIC ETHICS

A characteristic theme in the Akbarian psychological tradition is the correspondence of the macrocosm with the microcosm, *al-ʿālam al-kabīr* and *al-ʿālam al-ṣaghīr,* and sometimes referred to as *al-āfāq wa*

al-anfus (the 'horizons' and the souls) as in the
Qur'anic verse (41:53). The reference here is to the
manifestation of God's Names in the world and in
man. Taking the Prophetic hadith 'Allah has created
man upon His/his form' (*'alā ṣūratihi*), 'Allah' being
the Comprehensive Name (*ism al-jāmiʿ*), Ibn ʿArabī
states that God thus created man in the form of all
His Names. Although these Names are manifested
in all human beings, there is differentiation between
human qua human on the basis of the preponderance
of some Names over others in some people, as well
as the latent character of some Names in others. As
this *waṣf* (description) of the most Beautiful Names
was ascribed to the station of Adamic man,[20] he was
able to take upon himself the *amāna* (trust) that the
heavens and the earth refused to bear according to
the Qur'anic verse.[21]

Furthermore according to Ibn ʿArabī the asmā'
are the mulk proper to man, since there is no Divine
Name for which we do not possess a naṣīb (a
portion).[22] In Chapter 34 of the Futūḥāt, he takes
up the discussion of the amāna that has been taken
on by man as cited above. In reference to the hadith
regarding the creation of Adam (ʿalā ṣūratihi), he
states that although the *ḍamīr* (affixed pronoun) can
refer back to 'Adam' as the *nuẓẓār* might stipulate,
in reality it refers back to 'Allah' because of man's
assumption of the Divine Names. As in the *Iḥyā'*,[23]

---

20. Ibn ʿArabī, *al-Futūḥāt al-Makkiyya*, 4 vols. (Beirut: Dār Ṣādir, n.d.),
    2:170.6.

21. Q 33:73.

22. Ibn ʿArabi, *al-Futūḥāt*, 1:88, 2:124.

23. Ghazālī, *Iḥyā' ʿulūm al-dīn* (Jeddah: Dār al-Minhāj, 1432/2011),
    5:54.

Ibn ʿArabi cites the hadith qudsi (although generally considered inauthentic): 'My earth and My heavens cannot encompass Me, but the heart of My believing servant encompasses Me'.[24] For Ibn ʿArabī, this *siʿat bi iḍāfat al-yāʾ* (breadth by the relation of the added letter yāʾ) is the *ṣūra* (form) upon which man was created, as if Allah was saying, 'All My Names were not manifested except in the human plane (*nashʾat al-insāniyya*).' This is because 'And Adam was taught all the Names',[25] that is to say, the Divine Names from which all things in the cosmos were created and more importantly which the angels were not even given.

Whereas Sufi literature commonly stipulates that the Real manifests or epiphanizes Himself (*tajallī*) to the servant in accordance with that servant's spiritual capacity (*istiʿdād*), Ibn ʿArabī specifies that the case is not so. The case, rather, is that it is the servant that is 'manifested' to the Real in accordance with the form in which the Real manifests Himself to him.[26] The reception of the Real in the heart is in accordance with a predisposition or capacity, which itself is the result of a hidden theophany (*tajallī ghayb*), which bestows this capacity in the servant. When the Real then manifests Himself in the heart (tajallī shahāda), the heart thus recognizes Him as the Real or as *ilāh al-iʿtiqād* (the creedal deity) in accordance with the predisposition bestowed. The heart thus encompasses the Real in as far as He is

---

24. On the notion of the breadth of the heart, see Ibn ʿArabī, *Fuṣūṣ al-ḥikam*, ed. Abū al-ʿUlā al-ʿAfīfī (Beirut: Dār al-Kitāb al-ʿArabī, 1400/1980), Chapter 12, 119–21.
25. Q2:31.
26. Ibn ʿArabī, Fuṣūṣ, 1:120.

contained in the predispositional belief of the servant. This bestowal is in accordance with the Qur'anic verse 'Our Lord is He who bestows on everything its predis-position' (khalqahu).[27]

The *si'at* or breadth mentioned above is one that comes from the *ṣūra al-insāniyya* (the human form), so *bi al-ma'nā* (in its meaning), and not an outward one since the Qur'an mentions: 'Assuredly the creation of the heavens and the earth is greater than the creation of mankind, but most of mankind do not know this',[28] hence the ability of man to take on the *amāna* (trust) which they, the heavens and earth, were unable to take. Ibn ʿArabī continues to depict man in this chapter as a *nuskhat jāmi'a* (all encompassing divine copy), in that an aspect of the heavens and the earth are recapitulated, bi *wa-jhin mā* (from a particular perspective), in him who emerged upon the name Allah.[29]

The Perfect Man (*al-insān al-kāmil*), for Ibn ʿArabī, is represented in the Prophet (Allah bless him and give him peace), who said in the hadith: *Addabanī Rabbī fa aḥsana ta'dībī* ('My Lord taught me *adab*, and perfected it in me'). In Chapter 288 of the *Futūḥāt*,[30] Ibn ʿArabī expands on the notion of *jam'* (gathering together), identifying it as the first thing that Allah commanded for His servant, that is to say adab. He explains the derivation of the word *adab* from *ma'daba*, the coming together for a meal,

---

27. Q 20:50; Ibn ʿArabī, Fuṣūṣ, 1:121.

28. Q 40:57.

29. See also on the relation of the microcosm to the macrocosm, Ibn ʿArabī, *Futūḥāt*, Chapter 73, Question 143, 2 : 123.35.

30. Ibid., 2 : 640.

and so *adab* is the coming together of the Good (*al-khayr*). In an alternate version of the hadith given earlier, when the Prophet (Allah bless him and give him peace) states 'Verily Allah has taught me *adab*', Ibn ʿArabī comments that what the Prophet (Allah bless him and give him peace) means is 'Allah gathered together in me all the good things' (*jamiʿ al-khayrāt*), because the Prophet (Allah bless him and give him peace) then continues by saying *fa ḥassana adabī*, that is to say 'Allah made me a locus for everything that is beautiful'. So similarly for Ibn ʿArabī, man is told to gather that which is good, for Allah has only created him for gathering (*al-jamʿ*), and if he does so then he, the servant, will be felicitous and Allah will grant him everything that he has gathered.

The idea of *adab* as a scale of value that places all things in their rightful place is here maintained as the overriding scheme. In Chapter 445 of the *Futūḥāt*,[31] Ibn ʿArabī revisits the *Addabanī* hadith again, to state that there are two ways (whether for *awliyāʾ* or ordinary people) to know the station of creatures with God (*manāzil al-khalq*). The first is that given by *kashf* (unveiling) wherein the station that each group of people occupies with Allah is unveiled and one is able to deal with them respectively at the level required. The other path is through the committed practice (*mulāzama*) of Divine *adab* (*adab ilāhī*). This is described as being that which Allah has legislated for His servants through His prophets. So the *sharāʾiʿ* are the *ādāb* of Allah that have been laid down for His servants. He who is faithful to the truth of Allah's *sharʿ* can be considered as having

31. Ibid., 4 : 58.

been schooled in the *adab* of the Real (*ta'addaba bi adab al-Ḥaqq*) and to also know the Friends of God (*awliyā' al-Ḥaqq*). The servant who gathers together the good and fills his two hands (*bi yadayhi*) with it can be recognized as the one who has possession of Allah's *adab*.

When the Prophet (Allah bless him and give him peace) states in the hadith (addressing Allah): 'All that is Good is in Your Hands',[32] Ibn ʿArabī explains that if one wishes to identify the Good (*khayr*) here it is the gathering together of the noble character traits (*jimāʿmakārim al-akhlāq*) which are known by custom (*ʿurf*) and through the Shariʿah. The hadith is also important for Ibn ʿArabī's understanding of theodicy in its second half, 'And evil does not go back to You'.[33] In Chapter 385 of the *Futūḥāt*,[34] Ibn ʿArabī states that ignorance is ab-sence of knowledge and thus can have no reality (*amr wujūdī*), and the absence here is *sharr* (evil). The hadith of the Prophet (Allah bless him and give him peace) shows that evil is not ascribed to Allah, because evil is not ontologically real either (*amr wujūdī*). Since all that is ontologically real is Good, and all Good goes back to Allah the sole Agent (*lā fāʿil illā Allāh*), who is Absolute Good (*al-khayr al-maḥḍ*), evil cannot then be said to partake of the Real. Thus the Qur'an ascribes to Him the most Beautiful Names.[35] Evil is then something that arises from the manifest world

---

32. Ibn ʿArabī quotes half of the hadith that continues: *wa al-sharru laysa ilayka.*
33. See also Q 41 : 46, 10 : 108.
34. Ibn ʿArabī, *Futūḥāt*, 3:528.
35. Q 59 : 24.

but not from Allah,[36] the more real one is the less evil one becomes. Attachment to the Real is the attachment (*mulāzama*) to the Divine *Adab*, the Shariʿah. It is well to note that *ḥusn* (good) or *qubḥ* (evil) in relation to the station of man's actions is directly linked to the disobedience or obedience of the *aḥkām* of Allah. Beyond these, Ibn ʿArabī states that there is no binary distinction, but merely *ḥusn*.[37]

In his response to Question 45 of al-Ḥakīm al-Tirmidhī in Chapter 73, Ibn ʿArabī quotes the hadith: *uʿṭītu jawāmiʿ al-kalim*, which he describes as being in reference to the station of the giving of the Names to Adam[38], which the Prophet (Allah bless him and give him peace) most perfectly embodies, hence the *jamʿ*, whilst the *kalim* are the Names. In response to Question 46, which asks how many character traits were given to Adam, Ibn ʿArabī responds by quoting the hadith: 'Verily Allah has three hundred traits, he who assumes one of them will enter the Garden'. These traits are described as having been bestowed on Adam, their realization is not acquired by any good deeds but are bestowed by Allah as a gift.[39]

---

36. Ibn ʿArabī, *Futūḥāt*, 3:389.

37. Ibid., 3:403.

38. Q 21:31 (*wa ʿallama Ādama al-asmāʾa kullahā*).

39. Assuming them in this way is not possible since they are independently arising from divine theophanies in accordance with their number (*wa innamā hiya iʿdādāt bi anfusihā li tajalliyyāt ilāhiyya ʿalā ʿadadihā*). In *Sīrat al-awliyāʾ*, the tenth-century Sufi al-Ḥakīm al-Tirmidhī (d.295–300/905–910) refers to the character traits of Allah as numbering 117 traits following upon another reading of the hadith. See Muḥammad ibn ʿAlī al-Ḥakīm al-Tirmidhī, 'Sīrat al-awliyāʾ ', in *Thalāthat muṣannafāt li-al-Ḥakīm al-Tirmidhī*, ed. Bernd Radtke (Stuttgart: F. Steiner, 1992), 99, §128.

In Chapter 149 of the *Futūḥāt*,[40] Ibn ʿArabī states that *akhlāq* are *nuʿūt ilāhiyya* (Divine Attributes), all of them noble and all innate in man (*jibilla*). Ibn ʿArabī continues that those that are ignorant of the higher realities speak of their assumption by man and their trait being existent in Allah. So that in man they are assumed or acquired and are naturally present in Allah. This may be true in a metaphoric sense, however if they mean by assumption that at one point they do not possess the traits and then they assume them, then they have not understood that these are innate. The traits Ibn ʿArabī is referring to are the noble traits that the Sufis speak of cultivating, however he distinguishes two senses for them at the end of this chapter, one of them being that of the conventional meaning understood. The other sense he wishes to bring out is that the innate disposition is in man due to Adam being created upon His form. The traits are Allah's traits but not borrowed nor acquired in that sense since it is Allah who remains in possession of them as the Self-Existent. When we came into existence we came already possessing them, *fa lammā kunnā, kunnā bihā* (When we were existentiated, we possessed them).

As was stated above, *sub specie aeternitatis,* all that is brought into existence is *khayr,* however since there resides in the gradation of existence a concomitant delimitation of being, this 'absence' then entails evil. The world of forms around us, in one sense for Ibn ʿArabī, the phenomenal world or the world of *asbāb* (secondary causes), is a manifestation of the Names of Allah and can lead us

---

40. Ibn ʿArabī, *Futūḥāt*, 2:241.

to Him, *Musabbib al-asbāb* (the Causer of causes) or *Mukawwin al-asbāb* (the Creator of causes),[41] or else can be a veil taking us away from Him. This positive aspect in Ibn ʿArabī's writings for the world of causes is in sharp contrast to those ascetic Sufis who generally eschewed causes as being inferior and of no importance. Ibn ʿArabī establishes that in accordance with the Divine economy, so to speak, nothing that has been brought into existence lacks value, nor does it not lead one back to Allah, as in the verse 'Wheresoever you may turn, there is the face of God' (*wajhu Llāh*).[42] The Wajh is the Divine Names turned towards the created order, making of that order a warp woven with the weft of Divine significance of the effects of the Names, to be contemplated by the *adīb*. As Adamic man, this sense is brought out in the hadith: *man ʿarafa nafsahu faqad ʿarafa Rabbahu* ('Whosoever knows himself knows his Lord').

A point should be made finally regarding the different levels of man's servitude.[43] The first is *ʿubūda* (servitude), which is man's ontological state of conformity to the Divine Order (or one could say *aʿyān al-thābita*) without any possibility of disobedience. It is inalterable no matter the station that a man might reach on the spiritual path. The other is *ʿubūdiyya* (servanthood), which al-Jīlī

---

41. Ibid., 2 : 414.

42. Q 2 : 115.

43. This has been the subject of a masterly study by Michel Chodkiewicz, *Un Océan sans Rivage* (Paris: Seuil, 1992), translated by David Streight as, *An Ocean Without Shore: Ibn ʿArabî, The Book, and the Law* (Albany: State University of New York Press, 1993), 121–9. See also ʿAbd al-Karīm al-Jīlī, *al-Isfār ʿan risālat al-anwār fi mā yatajalla li ahl al-dhikr min al-anwār* (Beirut: Dār al-Kutub al-ʿIlmiyya, 1424/2004).

describes as remaining conscious of one's *'ubūda*, whilst in the abode of obligation or manifestation, to which one is obedient. It is such consciousness that leads to the perfection of *'ibāda* (worship). *'Ubūda*, needless to say, remains the same regardless of the actions of man in the world of manifestation, it cannot change, and it cannot be resisted nor avoided, hence it cannot be acquired nor assented to.

Epilogue

This has been an all too brief glimpse into Ibn 'Arabī's axiological notions of ethics, namely the ontological basis that he gives to *ḥusn* and *qubḥ*. In the deontological view, there is a separation made between the thing performed in itself and the command to do it. The command of the Legislator here makes it right or wrong rather than the act itself performed by the servant. Ibn 'Arabī in one sense reintegrates the ontological ground of the act with the Actor himself so that all acts are deemed to be part of the interplay of the Divine Names, and if the latter then Allah.

It was my intention to touch upon the notion that an approach to ethics from a metaphysical point of view in the Akbarian sense served to establish that the ontological approach to ethics is firmly rooted in our tradition. Although its explication is unlikely to be successfully rendered into an 'analytical' mould, it remains effective nevertheless in seeing off the Counter-Ontological objection since the Good can be defined objectively. The essential character of modern ethics is that it never rises beyond a pragmatic psychologism, in contrast to traditional ethics that is premised on a transcendental definition of the human being. The latter is an ontological matter, first and foremost, and thus within the domain of the science of metaphysics. Right ethics in this scheme stems from right theology, in turn providing a right economics and thus ensuring a right politics, when premises are declared, certain, and founded on an ontological order of reality.

9 789948 000938